Drum

Eagles

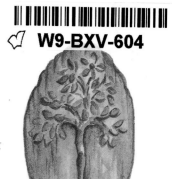

Fire Mark

Insectarium

Jelly Bean People

"Nevermore"

Opera

Phillies

Sampler

Tubing

Xmas

Yum!

Zschock

Art

Buggy

Clothespin

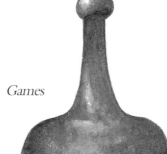

Games

Hex Sign

Key

Lightning

Mushrooms

Quaker

Rocky

U.S. Mint

Valley Forge

Wig

Journey Around

Philadelphia
from A to Z

Martha Day Zschock

COMMONWEALTH EDITIONS

Beverly, Massachusetts

ISBN-13: 978-1-933212-28-9
ISBN-10: 1-933212-28-4

For more information about the Philadelphia Mural Arts Program (MAP), please visit www.muralarts.org.

Visit Martha Zschock on the Web at www.journeyaround.com.

Published by Commonwealth Editions, 266 Cabot Street, Beverly, Massachusetts 01915.
Visit us on the Web at www.commonwealtheditions.com.

Printed in China.

10 9 8 7 6 5 4 3 2 1

To my wonderful family

And to teachers everywhere:
Thank you for all you do to inspire and encourage
your students, both young and old.
(Cheers to your retirement, Peg, Wayne, Trudy, Sue, and
Sarah. Thank you for all you have taught me!)

A special thank-you also to my patient publishers, Webster and Katie Bull!

"On the whole, I'd rather be in Philadelphia."

—*W. C. Fields*

Welcome to Philadelphia!

THIS IS THE CITY WHERE AMERICA BEGAN—where delegates met to declare their independence from Great Britain and where the U.S. Constitution was crafted. Philadelphia served as the country's first capital and has remained a vibrant center of culture throughout the life of the nation.

With visions of religious freedom for all, William Penn arrived in 1682. In the 1700's Benjamin Franklin helped develop many of the city's and the country's institutions. Philadelphia is home to a church that stands on the oldest piece of ground in the United States owned continuously by African Americans, and it has welcomed countless other racial and ethnic groups since then. The City of Brotherly Love is a worthy nickname for this diverse community.

Philadelphia is a city of neighborhoods, where musical styles echo off walls painted with colorful murals, where the smells of ethnic cooking—and juicy cheese steaks—entice and attract young and old. Come, there's much to see, to hear, and to eat! Let's take a journey around Philadelphia!

Wissahickon
Creek

Fairmount
Park

Philadelphia

Schuylkill
River

Center
City

Old City

Delaware River

Camden

New Jersey

N

W   E

S

Advice and Aphorisms appear in the almanack.

FEW PEOPLE IN HISTORY CAN CLAIM the accomplishments of Benjamin Franklin. He was a printer, scientist, publisher, inventor, congressional delegate, diplomat, postmaster, leader in the fight for independence, signer of the U.S. Constitution, and more. His dedication to serving others improved life for Philadelphians and all Americans. He helped establish a volunteer fire department, subscription library, and hospital, and he founded the University of Pennsylvania.

Franklin published clever advice like "Haste makes waste" in Poor Richard's Almanack.

Main: Ben Franklin statue, University of Pennsylvania
Inset: Franklin Court, Old City
Detail: "Ben Franklin, Craftsman," Center City

Beliefs bonded brothers.

WELCOME PARK

The names of the streets are mostly taken from the things that grow in the country, as Vine Street, Mulberry Street, Chestnut Street and the like.

PINE STREET

WILLIAM PENN, A QUAKER, FOUNDED PENNSYLVANIA in 1682 as a "Holy Experiment." His progressive ideas promised religious freedom, an elected government, trial by jury, and education for both boys and girls. Penn's principles inspired writers of the Constitution a century later. Penn's original plan for Philadelphia (the Greek word for "city of brotherly love") is still evident in the city's broad streets and the parks in each of its corners.

Main: "Love" Statue, Kennedy Plaza
Inset: Welcome Park
Detail: Wampum Belt, Atwater Kent Museum

A wampum belt given to William Penn by the local Leni Lanape represents a "chain of friendship."

Constitution creators crafted the country's creed.

IN 1787, THE FOUNDING FATHERS met in Philadelphia to write the U.S. Constitution. Providing the structure of American government, the Constitution divided power into three branches: executive, legislative, and judiciary. The Constitution did have one notable failing: it did not end slavery. This led to the Civil War in 1861. The National Constitution Center explains how the Constitution continues to shape our lives.

Personal freedoms, like freedom of speech, were guaranteed by the Bill of Rights in 1791.

Main: National Constitution Center
Inset: Signers' Hall, National Constitution Center
Detail: "The Signer," Old City

Dignity and dedication develop dreams.

Blessed are the peacemakers for they shall be called the children of GOD

MATTHEW 5:9

MURAL PAINTED BY PRIOR MURAL ARTS PROGRAM

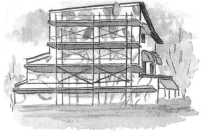

IMAGINE BEING *ALLOWED* TO PAINT ON WALLS! In 1984, the Philadelphia Anti-Graffiti Network was formed to encourage graffiti writers to beautify neighborhoods. Due to the success of the Mural Arts Program (MAP), Philadelphia has more than 2,500 murals celebrating its diversity, culture, and history. Through free art education and mentorship programs, MAP makes young people feel proud of themselves and their communities.

Main: "Peace Wall," by Jane Golden
Inset: "Common Threads," by Meg Saligman
Detail: "Seeds of the Future," by Donald Gensler

Murals can be as large as the eight-story work "Common Threads."

E merald
acres
enhance the
environment.

PHILADELPHIA'S "BACKYARD," FAIRMOUNT PARK, celebrated its 150th birthday in 2005 and proves that some things keep getting better with age. Originally established with five acres along the Schuylkill River, the park has grown to an amazing 9,200-acre system that includes parks throughout the city. No Philadelphia resident lives farther than one mile from a park!

Imagine a mansion that's all yours to play in! You'll find it at Smith Memorial Playground and Playhouse.

Main: Japanese House, Fairmount Park
Inset: Philadelphia Zoo
Detail: Ann Newman Giant Wooden Slide, Smith Memorial Playground and Playhouse

Flowers, flags, and fountains line Franklin's fairway.

Rodin Museum

BENJAMIN FRANKLIN PARKWAY, connecting Center City with the Fairmount Park system, is compared to the Champs Elysées in Paris. The grand boulevard with its museums, scientific institutions, city buildings, and cultural centers was the vision of city planners who began making their dream a reality before 1920. Flags in alphabetical order along the parkway represent the nations whose people live in Philadelphia.

Main: Benjamin Franklin Parkway
Inset: Swann Fountain, Logan Square
Details: Parkway attractions

The parkway is the perfect setting for Fourth of July fireworks!

Academy of Natural Sciences

I ♥ 2 READ

Franklin Institute

Free Library of Philadephia

Gleaming gems grace grand galleries.

COVERING TEN ACRES, the Philadelphia Museum of Art holds 225,000 works of art spanning over 2,000 years. Nearby, the Pennsylvania Academy of the Fine Arts is the country's oldest art school and museum of fine arts. The Rodin Museum showcases work by the French sculptor who beautifully captured the movements and emotions of his models. It's fun to compare artwork in books with the real thing!

At the Brandywine River Museum, volunteers create fanciful "critter" ornaments during the holidays.

Main: Philadelphia Museum of Art
Inset: Pennsylvania Academy of the Fine Arts
Details: Critters, Brandywine River Museum

History happened here!

INDEPENDENCE VISITOR CENTER

PENN'S LANDING

We the People

THE NEIGHBORHOOD SURROUNDING INDEPENDENCE HALL is "America's most historic mile." Here the country was born. Located between north and south, Philadelphia was a logical meeting place during the Revolutionary era and served as the nation's capital from 1790 to 1800. Established on July 4, 1956, the Independence National Historical Park preserves buildings and artifacts that tell the story of the nation's beginning.

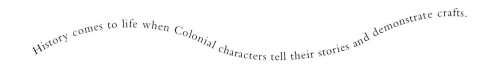

History comes to life when Colonial characters tell their stories and demonstrate crafts.

Main: Old City
Inset: Independence Visitor Center, Old City
Details: Colonial Guides

Ideas of Independence inspired the Founders.

INDEPENDENCE HALL, originally the Pennsylvania capitol, was the stage for events that changed American history. Here delegates came together, angered by the unfair actions of the British. Here George Washington was appointed commander in chief of the Continental Army, the Declaration of Independence was signed, and the Constitution was adopted. Here today, millions of visitors see where America was born.

Thomas Jefferson drafted the Declaration of Independence in rooms he rented in Declaration House.

Main: Independence Hall
Inset: Assembly Room, Independence Hall
Detail: Declaration House

Jersey's just a jog away!

Adventure Aquarium,
Children's Garden,
Battleship New Jersey,
Walt Whitman's
House

SPEED LIMIT 35

2 LANES TO N.J.

NO TOL
THIS D

SCHOOL BUS

SINCE 1688, FERRIES HAVE LINKED Philadelphia and New Jersey. Today, tourists can board a ferry at Penn's Landing to discover Camden, New Jersey's lively waterfront. A five-story sunflower peeks out from the Children's Garden as you dock. At the new Adventure Aquarium, sharks surround visitors and hippos bask in an African river. Journey on to Battleship New Jersey, a museum that floats!

Main: Benjamin Franklin Bridge
Inset: Camden, New Jersey
Detail: Camden River Sharks

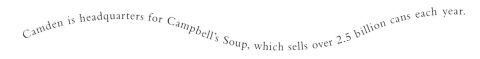

Camden is headquarters for Campbell's Soup, which sells over 2.5 billion cans each year.

Kettles hung in Colonial kitchens.

COLONIAL PEOPLE HANDCRAFTED items needed for everyday life. Blacksmiths made cooking utensils, coopers built barrels, and cobblers crafted shoes. Today we learn about life long ago by studying things people made then. The Mercer Museum displays a vast collection of tools representing Early American trades. You can also see where craftspeople once lived by strolling down Elfreth's Alley, the country's oldest continually occupied residential street.

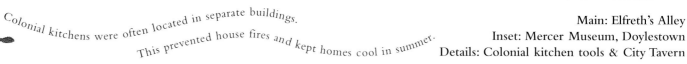

Colonial kitchens were often located in separate buildings.
This prevented house fires and kept homes cool in summer.

Main: Elfreth's Alley
Inset: Mercer Museum, Doylestown
Details: Colonial kitchen tools & City Tavern

Let liberty ring loudly through the land.

THE LIBERTY BELL IS A SYMBOL of freedom recognized worldwide. It probably announced the first public reading of the Declaration of Independence and traveled around the country to help rebind the nation after the Civil War. It cracked soon after it was made, was recast, and cracked again! Like liberty, the bell is fragile. The Liberty Museum explores ways to protect and celebrate our diverse society created by freedom.

Main: The Liberty Bell
Inset: National Liberty Museum
Detail: Abolitionist symbol

The Liberty Bell was a symbol for abolitionists because of its inscription, "Proclaim liberty throughout all the land unto all the inhabitants thereof."

STRUTTING TO THEIR UNOFFICIAL THEME SONG, "O' Dem Golden Slippers," by James Bland, mummers welcome the New Year with a lavish parade. The tradition began in the late seventeenth century when Swedish settlers brought to the New World their simple Christmas custom of visiting friends. Over the years, the festivities expanded to include costumes and music as other immigrants joined the celebration.

From the Fourth of July parade to Chinese New Year celebrations, there's always something exciting going on!

Main: Mummers Museum, South Philly
Inset: Divisions of Mummers
Details: Happy Fourth of July!

Neighborhoods define urban nature.

WITH ABOUT TWO HUNDRED NEIGHBORHOODS, Philadelphia is known as the "City of Neighborhoods." In early days, different cultures, classes, and religions lived and worshiped side by side. As the city grew, each neighborhood began to reflect the special traditions of its inhabitants. Philadelphia has developed an atmosphere all its own, in which the city continually strives for the tolerance of its founders.

Main: Philadelphia Row Houses
Inset: Italian Market
Details: Eighth Street and Lehigh Avenue

Kids toss worn-out sneakers over telephone wires at Eighth Street and Lehigh Avenue.

O ld Order Amish obey the Ordnung.

WITHOUT MODERN CONVENIENCES like electricity, phones, or cars, Amish life may seem strange. The Amish, who began arriving in Pennsylvania about three centuries ago, obey the Ordnung, a list of rules that tells them how to live. Although simple, theirs is a life many choose. Amish children grow up in nurturing homes, and most choose to remain in their supportive community as adults.

In most Amish communities, married men grow beards (but not mustaches) and women never cut their hair.

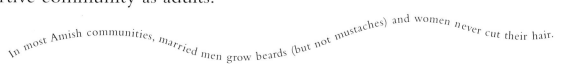

Main: Lancaster County
Inset: Amish Quilts, Lancaster Quilt & Textile Museum
Detail: Amish Family

Philly food pleases the palate.

ALTHOUGH PHILADELPHIA IS RECOGNIZED for its restaurants, ethnic food, and farm-fresh produce, the city's most popular delicacies are its own unique creations. Philadelphia is known for the best cheese steaks, water ices, soft pretzels, hoagies, and tasty kakes anywhere. Philadelphians all have their own opinions about who makes the best cheese steaks: Pat's or Geno's, Geno's or Pat's— or Jim's?! You be the judge!

Main: Food Court, Reading Terminal Market
Inset: Pat's & Geno's, South Philly
Detail: There's nothing like a Philadelphia pretzel!

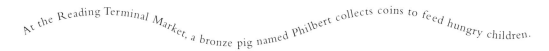

At the Reading Terminal Market, a bronze pig named Philbert collects coins to feed hungry children.

Quilts
of color
cover Quaker
farms.

NUMEROUS BOTANICAL GARDENS, arboretums, and nature preserves grace Philadelphia and the surrounding countryside. Longwood Gardens grew from a Quaker farm to a horticultural masterpiece under the tender, loving care of Pierre S. du Pont, who combined technology with gardening science. Today Longwood has 1,050 outdoor acres and 20 indoor gardens. In March, the annual Philadelphia Flower Show is a welcome sign of spring for winter-weary folks.

The Pennsylvania state bird is the ruffed grouse. The state flower is the mountain laurel.

Main: Longwood Gardens, Kennett Square
Inset: Philadelphia Flower Show, mid-March
Details: Mountain Laurel and Ruffed Grouse

Rumors, not records, recognize Ross.

① Fold an 8.5 x 10" piece of paper in half

8.5"

5"

② Keep folded and crease on dotted lines.

③ Fold Left corner from vertical crease to meet the horizontal crease

④ Left edge

Fold left corner back to left edge until edges meet, then crease.

R

⑤ Bring the Right corner to the left and crease along the fold line.

⑥ Bring Right corner to the fold line so edges match and fold along blue line.

Fold line

R

⑦ Tricky Part!... Cut at the angle shown above. Unfold the top piece and...

Voila! you are a Star!

IN 1776, BETSY ROSS SEWED the first American flag—or so the story goes. Historians rely on "primary sources" such as diaries and letters to piece together the past. No such evidence has been found to prove the tale of Betsy Ross. Some question the story that she changed the star from six points to five with a single snip. But here's how you can do it.

Betsy Ross's and George Washington's pews at Christ Church were across from each other.

Main: Betsy Ross House, Old City
Inset: Clever!
Detail: Christ Church

BOATHOUSE ROW, WITH ITS BEAUTIFUL LIGHTS, is home to the "Schuylkill Navy," a group of rowing clubs founded in 1858. The city's famous waterworks and dam were built downstream from 1812 to 1821, creating a perfect location for rowing. College students from across the country look forward to the annual Dad Vail Regatta, the largest annual collegiate crew races in the United States.

Philadelphia developed the country's first municipal waterworks after yellow fever struck in 1793.

Main: Boat House Row
Inset: John B. Kelly, "The Rower," Kelly Drive
Detail: Fairmount Waterworks and Interpretive Center

Topping the tip sparked debate.

CITY HALL DOMINATES the centermost of five public squares in William Penn's original city plan. Designed to be the tallest building in the world, it was surpassed before it was completed. A 37-foot statue of Penn gazes upon the city from the front tower. Built in 1987, Liberty Place was first to break a long-standing gentlemen's agreement that no city building would top Penn's hat.

Main: Philadelphia skyline
Inset: William Penn, City Hall
Detail: Alexander Calder's "Eagle" once visited the city

Alexander Milne Calder designed all of City Hall's sculpture, including the Penn statue.

BLACKSMITH SHOP 1791

1ST CHURCH

ROUGHCAST 1805

2ND CHURCH

CHURCH AFRICAN

EPISCOPAL METHODIST

RICHARD ALLEN

FOUNDER 1760 – 1831

4TH CHURCH

3RD CHURCH

AT PRESENT 1889

MOTHER BETHEL

BRICK CHURCH 1841

Underground Railroad ushers hid fugitive slaves.

THE UNDERGROUND RAILROAD was neither underground nor a railroad. It was a secret network that aided enslaved Africans escaping to the North and Canada. "Conductors" guided "passengers" (slaves) to hiding places called "stations." With a large number of antislavery supporters, Philadelphia was an important stop on the "railroad." The city's African American Museum was first of its kind to showcase achievements of black Americans.

Over 500 black dolls at the Philadelphia Doll Museum show changes in African American life.

Main: Mother Bethel AME Church
Inset: African American Museum
Detail: Philadelphia Doll Museum

V intage vessels reveal adventurous voyages.

Lying between the Schuylkill River and the Delaware River, which connects to the Atlantic Ocean, Philadelphia has always been an important port. The Independence Seaport Museum explores the city's maritime heritage. Younger sailors enjoy sailing toy boats at Please Touch Museum. It is a challenge to keep rivers clean while using them for recreation, industry, and trade.

Main: *Olympia*, Independence Seaport Museum
Inset: Please Touch Museum
Detail: Swann Fountain, Logan Circle

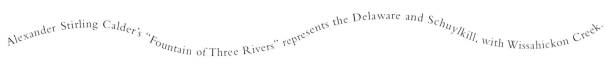

Alexander Stirling Calder's "Fountain of Three Rivers" represents the Delaware and Schuylkill, with Wissahickon Creek.

War of the wills weathered the winter.

NAKED AND STARVING AS THEY ARE WE CANNOT ENOUGH ADMIRE THE INCOMPARABLE PATIENCE AND FIDELITY OF THE SOLDIERY

DURING THE REVOLUTIONARY WAR, many Colonists joined the Continental Army in the fight for independence from Great Britain. In 1777, the British captured Philadelphia, largest city in the colonies. Keeping an eye on the British, General George Washington and his weary soldiers went into winter quarters at nearby Valley Forge. Despite terrible hardships, the troops persevered. Honing their skills, they emerged with renewed confidence, ready for the battles ahead.

Valley Forge looks idyllic, but the visitor center and reenactments help visitors experience what life was like during the long winter of 1777–78.

Main: Cabin, Valley Forge
Inset: National Memorial Arch, Valley Forge
Detail: Reenactment, Valley Forge

EXperts **X**exude exciting sounds.

Joe Frazier's Gym
The African Heritage Center
The Liacouras Center
The Legendary Blue Horizon
Jeanne Ruddy Dance
The Pennsylvania Academy of Fine Arts
Prince Music Theater
Academy of Music
Opera Company of Philadelphia
Merriam Theater
Kimmel Center for the Performing Arts
Brandywine Workshop Center for the Visual Arts
Philadelphia Clef Club

Philadelphia Doll Museum
Conwell Dance Theater
Rock Hall at Temple University
New Freedom Theatre
Fabric Workshop and Museum
Asian Arts Initiative
Philadelphia Music Alliance
Wilma Theater
University of the Arts Gershman Hall
Phila. Arts Bank
Pennsylvania Ballet
The Ballet Center

PHILADELPHIA HAS A RICH MUSICAL HISTORY that includes gospel, blues, jazz, rock, and hip-hop. More than three dozen theaters, schools, and cultural sites line the Avenue of the Arts district. The Kimmel Center is home to the Philadelphia Orchestra and other musical companies. Strings for Schools and the Philadelphia Music Alliance bring music to area students. Clef Club, founded by great black jazz musicians, teaches kids about jazz.

Main: Kimmel Center for the Performing Arts
Inset: Avenue of the Arts, Broad Street
Detail: Walk of Fame

More than 100 bronze plaques on the "Walk of Fame" honor Philadelphia musicians.

Yippee, yay, and hip hip hooray!

PHILADELPHIA IS ONE OF THE FEW CITIES in America to have a team and separate stadium for each major professional sport. Fans recall the glory days when the Eagles, Phillies, Flyers, and 76ers all played for championships. They also look forward to college games in the area. And the spirit of Rocky from the 1977 film about a Philadelphia boxer lives on!

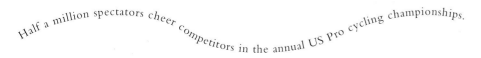

Half a million spectators cheer competitors in the annual US Pro cycling championships.

Main: Phillie Phanatic, Citizens Bank Park
Inset: "Rocky," A. Thomas Schomberg Sculptor, Wachovia Center
Detail: US Pro Cycling Championships

ZAP!

SOARING OVER THE DELAWARE RIVER, the Benjamin Franklin Bridge welcomes visitors to Philadelphia with an awesome view of the city and the energy of Isamu Noguchi's lightning-bolt statue. The statue is a tribute to Franklin's experiment in which he conducted electricity from the sky by flying a kite with a key attached during a thunderstorm. The Franklin Institute honors his memory and celebrates scientific discovery.

Main: Franklin Square
Inset: Ben Franklin, Franklin Institute Science Museum
Detail: One of Ben's many inventions

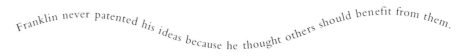

Franklin never patented his ideas because he thought others should benefit from them.

Drum

Eagles

Fire Mark

Insectarium

Jelly Bean People

"Nevermore"

Opera

Phillies

Sampler

Tubing

Xmas

Yum!

Zschock

Art

Buggy

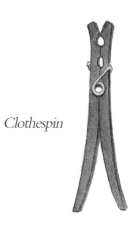

Clothespin

Games

Hex Sign

Key

Lightning

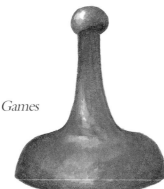

Mushrooms

Quaker

Rocky

U.S. Mint

Valley Forge

Wig